I0483001

TABLE OF CONTENTS

The Psychology of Sales
Using Behavioral Science to Influence Buyers
©Copyright 2013 by Dr. Harry Jay

DISCLAIMER AND TERMS OF USE AGREEMENT:

(Please Read This Before Using This Book)

This information is for educational and informational purposes only. The content is not intended to be a substitute for any professional advice, diagnosis, or treatment.

The author and publisher of this book and the accompanying materials have used their best efforts in preparing this book.

The author and publisher make no representation or warranties with respect to the accuracy, applicability, fitness, or completeness of the contents of this book. The information contained in this book is strictly for educational purposes. Therefore, if you wish to apply ideas contained in this book, you are taking full responsibility for your actions.

The author and publisher disclaim any warranties (express or implied), merchantability, or fitness for any particular purpose. The author and publisher shall in no event be held liable to any party for any direct, indirect, punitive, special, incidental or other consequential damages arising directly or indirectly from any use of this material, which is provided "as is", and without warranties. As always, the advice of a competent legal, tax, accounting, medical or other professional should be sought where applicable.

The author and publisher do not warrant the performance, effectiveness or applicability of any sites listed or linked to in this book. All links are for information purposes only and are not warranted for content, accuracy or any other implied or explicit purpose. No part of this may be copied, or changed in any format, or used in any way other than what is outlined within this course under any circumstances. Violators will be prosecuted.

This book is © Copyrighted by ePubWealth.com.

Introduction

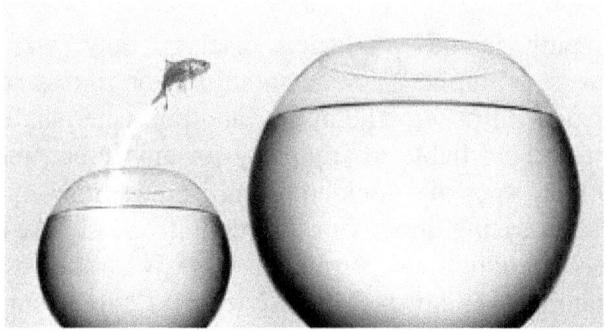

Psychological Phenomena - People Are People, no matter how complicated they may seem, and they all operate on a common psychological framework. Buyers use this framework to do just about everything, including buying from your company. The following encompasses a set of standard psychological phenomena, which are involved in all types of sales:

Following the Herd

A buyer's judgment is highly influenced by and dependent on, the collective judgment of groups of others. This means they will often make judgments that they believe are entirely his/her own, but in reality they are based on what other people are doing! For example: they may go out and decide to buy something, or take a trip somewhere, but that decision is most likely highly influenced by their observing, ~~or~~ reading about, or hearing about, other people doing the exact same thing. And they will often avoid things that most other people avoid. In fact, there are very many instances when they will adopt a group's judgment over their own! What this means is that you should have as many features, within your sales presentation, which allow buyers to contribute to, feel, and be influenced by, group opinions. For example, you must have testimonials. Depending on your presentation, other things you should consider adding are statistics and surveys. All these allow buyers to contribute to the group thought and be influenced by it.

Authority Is Always Listened to and Followed
People listen, unquestioningly, to authoritative figures ESPECIALLY MEN. If you hold anyone in high regard as an authority, you will usually, unquestioningly listen, and do as they say. Think about your doctor, lawyer, and sports coach. These people can tell you to do what most people can't, and you will almost always do it without questioning it. This means that your presentation should have someone or some organization of recognized authority, in that field, saying something positive about your product or service.

It doesn't have to be famous people, just authority heads. For example, a travel service can have a review by some magazine and a vitamin store can have some comments from doctors. Note: We will discuss later in detail how men view authority differently than women.

Small Leads to Big
If someone came up to you and asked you for your agreement on some major issue, they are more likely to get a "no" from you than if they came up to you, and led you on with a series of much smaller issues that you can easily agree on, building to the major issue. THIS IS IMPORTANT: ALWAYS BEGIN A SALES PRESENTATION FROM A POSITION OF AGREEMENT. THE BUYER SEES YOU AS "THE

ENEMY" AND HE/SHE THINKS THEIR JOB IS TO SAY "NO"! ALSO, USE AN INCREMENTAL APPROACH, STEP-BY-STEP TO REACH A CLOSING CONCLUSION. Getting people to agree to a major issue is a lot easier if you first give them related, but smaller, issues that they can automatically agree to. One way to use this in your business is to provide a free trial. It is easy to get someone to try something free. After that, it is much easier to get them to upgrade to a full-service version. Another thing you could do is to ask questions that most people will answer "yes" to, spread out within your sales pitch. They must be questions related to the product or service. That build up of several related, but easy, yes answers, make it much easier to get the final yes to buy.

Unfinished Business
Most people are quite disturbed by tasks, or events, that are incomplete, or unfinished. You know how you hate it when those TV shows stop somewhere in the middle of a juicy plot, only to tell you that they will be continued at the same time next week? It disturbs your mind so much that you make it a point of catching the next show. And, on the next show they do the exact same thing! Even in your life, when you have incomplete tasks, you keep thinking about them until you complete them. It is easier for people to remember and stay focused on incomplete tasks. There are many ways you can apply this to your marketing. Your sales presentation should lead the buyer from one page to the next, using this phenomenon. NEVER COMPLETE A THOUGHT ON ONE PAGE. ALWAYS CONTINUE IT ONTO THE NEXT PAGE. This small and seemingly insignificant idea actually controls the buyer. And, NEVER give the buyer the

complete sales presentation! Hand it to him/her page-by-page, so that they cannot read ahead and formulate objections. A person reading is NOT listening.

Cognitive Dissonance

Calm down, I sometimes need to use big words. In plain English, this means that people hate it when their beliefs are inconsistent with their actions. They won't rest until they resolve that conflict by changing their thoughts, beliefs, or actions. One way to use this in marketing is to get someone to make an easy decision, and then get them to take actions on their own, so that they can prove to themselves that they made the right decision. People usually want to validate that they made the right choice. Another way to work this is to give them that validation early on, so that when it comes to the sale, they will have already eliminated their dissonance and they will buy to reinforce their belief.

Conforming to the Herd

In a happy room, most people get happy. In a sad room, most people get sad. People conform to the emotions of the group or environment. That is why casinos and top retail outlets pay psychologists to create an emotional atmosphere of carefree spending, or something similar, which will cause emotions that lead to spending. Color is also a big part to how people respond. Hospitals employ soft pastels to calm people down. Have a look at your sales presentation. What emotion does it convey? A presentation's text, prose, colors, graphics, and quality can make or break a sale just from the emotional angle.

Needs Satisfaction

Whenever people buy something, they do it to get some need fulfilled, and/or to eliminate some problem. Simple.

Even if you go out to buy a boomerang, the principle is the same. There is a need you wish to fulfill, such as exercise, amusement, discovery, fun. You may also be looking to eliminate something else, such as boredom. Examine your products and services, and forget all the hype that you enjoy about your product. Forget the way you love that super-cool feature you built in. Just think on the needs level. Find out what needs a buyer wants to fulfill, and what they would want to eliminate. Needs are not features. THINK BENEFITS! Needs are things like saving time, spending time with the family, knowing something, or achieving success. That is what you will be selling. You only mention the features as a side item, to seal the decision logically, but the decision to buy will be based on emotions and needs, which are BENEFITS.

Surprise, Free and Casual Works
Most people ignore advertising or direct calls to buy something. They get defensive initially. They even learn to automatically 'not see' advertising. I am sure that your brain somehow blocks out all those ads, and only very rarely, do you even notice what is really in them. Why? Well, because your brain can see the ad coming! It has all the cues that make it look like an ad, and it is shut out. What if it did not look like an ad? Perhaps it looked like content that you would be interested in reading, or a cartoon you like? You would see it and read it! What this means is that your sales presentation, and everything else, should have nothing that smells of advertising. ALWAYS THINK BENEFITS! Eventually you must ask for the sale **(Yes, You Must Clearly Ask Your Client to Buy, But Only, at the Right Time)**. However, until the point where all your prospects emotional and logical requirements have been fulfilled, you must look like a

free information service, or at least provide useful information along the way, even in your product information sheets. You must be the opposite of an advertisement. An ad tells you quickly about the product, its features, and screams at you to buy. The opposite is a useful information resource. That keeps the prospect calm, gives them something useful, while subtly leading to the sale. ALWAYS INCLUDE A FACT SHEET IN YOUR PRESENTATION, WHICH IS COMPLETELY GEARED TO YOUR BUYER'S NEEDS. Only at the point of sale is the sale asked for, very clearly and bluntly. With this strategy you will be ignored far less, and the client will read your material much more. Give people free, instantly useful information, and entertainment; let that lead subtly, but persistently, to the sale. Keep it casual. You should also try to use something that people have never seen before. Surprise them in this way and they will pay attention. For example, when making a presentation, don't do it like everyone else does. Use a design trick that people haven't seen before. A GOOD EXAMPLE IS WHAT I HAVE SAID PREVIOUSLY: HAND THE PROPOSAL TO THEM ONE PAGE AT A TIME! By the way, a good reason to offer something free and useful is that it allows you to be a part of your prospect's life. Once you have entered their life, you will be more readily accepted, and can then work up to the sale.

Customers Make Decisions On Complicated Personal Psychological Levels
Have you have ever wondered what they are? Below are several specific, unspoken psychological sales factors. If you are upset about not closing sales, or going crazy trying to build strong customer relationships, consider

9

whether any of the following factors might apply to your particular situation.

Reputation

The customer's personal career reputation is more important than your product performance, price, quality, guarantees, service, or any number of excuses and free lunches. The old saying is, "You are known by the friends you keep." What is your reputation? If you do not have a reputation, what does it seem like?

Trust

Your customer may know that there are better vendors for the job. But, you have the business because he knows that you will never get him in trouble with his superiors, or take credit for his work.

Habit

Fast schedules and time constraints force customers to fill in the blanks. A customer makes decisions a certain way because it 'feels right,' and has caused him the least amount of pain in his organization in the past. The customer does not consciously know why he makes decisions, behaves, or even dresses the way he does. Here is a good example ... ever meet someone who does not deal well with problems after 2:00 pm? Hint: It's easier to change your presentation time, than it is to change their nature.

Clubs

A customer organization will have a core of 'club members'. Membership in the club speaks of achievement, loyalty, and privilege. One member's decision over-rules any non-member's decision.

Nobodies

Beware of a customer who emulates a superior's authority or style. Others may resent their behavior, and perhaps their recommendations.

Perspective
Sales people think of scientists and say, "Can't I get a simple yes, or no?" Sales people are trained to think positively. Scientists think of sales people and say, "Lacks substance." Scientists are trained to think of all of the angles.

Image
Is your customer management material? He will want to highlight and draw attention to his dedication and sense of urgency. For example, he may call a weekend or 5:00 am meeting, regardless if the time for such a meeting is logical or required by the actual work.

Politics
Some in an organization make decisions based only on personal gain. They rule against your idea when the organization may have something to gain by success; but they personally have nothing to gain from taking the risk. In the minds of these people, a possible benefit to the organization seems bigger if it results in their personal gain.

Branding
Your first job, with a new prospect, is to make your name known. Does your prospect remember you? Really? Face it, after a few weeks, some busy executives might forget they've talked with you -- or met with you -- entirely. Find ways to keep in touch with your customers.

Subordinates

You will need help from subordinates. Don't forget to give them the time and respect that they really deserve. Consider the receptionist who won't let you speak to the manager, and tells him that you are a rude jerk. The quiet laboratory technician may have poor social skills, but could accomplish significant things with your product. Your customer's top managers may communicate, and dress well, but might not fully understand your product. So, guess whose opinion they rely on in the final analysis (hint: not yours)? Knowing about psychological factors may help to keep you in your customer's good wishes, keep you out of trouble, and increase your odds of closing sales.

"One of the reasons apples rot is that they are taken off the tree."

(It is so very important to stay focused)

Chapter 1 – Closing Techniques

One unique aspect of industrial sales is sales closing techniques: You are at the end of your meeting. On the other side of the table is the purchasing director of a Fortune 500 corporation. He has over 30 years of experience in purchasing and negotiation. He has a photographic memory and knows your market better than you. You are finished describing your company, your product, and your capabilities. You know you can meet his requirements better than your competition, but maybe your price is a bit higher. Using one of the most important rules in negotiating, he is perfectly quiet, waiting for you to speak. Unfortunately, your co-workers are in the meeting, also staring at you, impatiently, waiting for you to speak. How do you cross to the other side of the tracks, without getting hit by the train?

Start by recognizing that one of the unique aspects of industrial sales is in sales closing techniques. The industrial sales process is **Unlike** retail sales (we will come back to this in a moment).

Your customer will (i) have a different attitude and (ii) have a different decision process. In other words, selling a $500,000 technical product to a corporation differs from, selling a home entertainment system to a family.

The key in industry sales is finding a way to close with prospects that have extensive training, and experience, in product purchasing and in negotiation. THINK BENEFITS!

Closing Sales in Retail Selling
We have all heard about using sales closing techniques in retail sales. In retail sales, as many as a dozen closing techniques may be successfully applied, in A SINGLE MEETING! However, here is the dictionary definition of sales closing suicide, in market-to-market selling:

Using a dozen sales closes on an experienced senior purchasing manager"! For example, have you heard any of the following sales closes in gift shops, or car lots?

You are right: "I can understand your hesitation; the color is certainly not exactly what you had in mind.

Many of our customers felt the same way, until their friend received this gift. They discovered this color to be very popular."

Competitor endorsement: "Mr. Smith, as we discussed earlier, this is a popular color. In fact, your neighbor Mr. Jones purchased one yesterday."

A choice: "Mr. Smith would you like the blue color or the red color?"

Bluff called: "Mr. Smith, if I can get you the yellow color, would you take it?"

The impending doom: "Mr. Smith, please come and see us after you and your wife talk about the color. But, one of the reasons I wanted to wrap this up today for you is that the price increases tomorrow."

The crowded room: "One of the reasons I wanted to wrap this up for you today is that we only have five blue items left in inventory."

Logical: "If I can prove to you, without a doubt, that blue will work, will you give it a try?"

The challenge: "Mr. Smith, I don't think you will need the blue color. Can I show you the red color?"

Value added: "Mr. Smith, we have developed customer financing, so you won't have to worry about that."

Kick the Tires: "Mr. Smith, it looks like you are serious about this, but have some doubts. I'll tell you what, buy it and take it home for a couple of days. If I'm wrong, if you aren't satisfied, for any reason, bring it back for a full refund."

Pre-Close: "If you buy this model, what kind of speakers would you plan to use with it?"

An assumption: "Mr. Smith, where would you like this delivered?"

Luxury: "Treat yourself to something nice today, and give us a try."

Reverse: "Mr. Smith, now that it's over, could I ask just one question? Why wouldn't you buy from me?"

A salesperson selects a particular close based on the situation and the personalities involved. The customer's response to a close, must be followed-up on, appropriately. These closes are only a select few examples. There are, literally, entire books written on sales closes.

An experienced car, or insurance, salesperson, may use between, six and a dozen closes, on a single prospect -- in a SINGLE MEETING. The experienced, successful, retail salesperson uses sales closes as a surgeon uses a scalpel. Sales closes are selected to, gradually build, uncomfortable feelings in the prospect.

The best retail sales closing expert, in the world, taught me the following about sales closing techniques, "You put your finger on the prospect's eye. So gradually, so gently, he doesn't blink." The prospect finally buys if only to end these uncomfortable feelings, caused by the closing techniques.

Closing Sales in Industry, or Market-To-Market Selling
It is important to understand how the excessive use of sales' closes may drive some trained and experienced industrial prospects away from the purchase of your technical product.

It's simple: The prospect realizes that he must answer to others in his organization -- or get rid of a trusted vendor -- which is less comfortable than your best closing techniques. He uses any one of dozens of techniques to postpone his decision; then he stops returning your calls. Industrial customers have a decision process, which helps to prevent impulse decisions, fraud, or theft, and to include others in the organization.

Sorry, but this is an unavoidable fact. Senior industrial purchasing agents have extensive formal training and experience in negotiation. They have long-term business relationships with some of their current vendors. Industrial customers may be under pressure from **sales psychology.**

Worse than appearing transparent and thoughtless, your excessive repetition of sales closes may permanently alienate your prospect. On the road to pitching to the decision maker, you will be required to first pitch to others.

The decision maker may require certain steps for evaluating your product, such as: literature, meetings with subordinates, sample evaluations, process trials, price negotiations, and comparisons to competitive products.

They may use you; perhaps invite you in only to accumulate additional data that justifies their current supplier. You must contend with advanced corporate purchasing tactics. Where do you start?

First, realize that closing should be a way of working, not a script. Begin by understanding all of the steps that the organization will require to complete the sale. Then, agree on what you will need to accomplish, at the current step, and how you would be permitted to move forward to the next step.

In other words, pre-qualify the customer's needs. This pre-qualification is basically your close -- done in advance! Your job is now to reach a mutual agreement that satisfies the customer's objectives; clearing a step, allowing you to move step by step, towards a check that clears the bank.

Believe it or not, you still have not closed. You will close only when your customer is completely satisfied. What's better than closing on a bank check? How about one of the greatest aspects of industry business: repeat orders?

My philosophy is to use one sales closing technique during any single meeting, or phone conversation.

Using too many closes in industrial product sales is a typical mistake; but not using any is another mistake. Using one close during a meeting will help to move a deal forward.

Using two closes may be helpful, in very few cases.

But, using three or more, seems very risky to me -- in business-to-business product sales.

Furthermore, I use more of a conversational close, not a scripted close.

For example, there are some purchasing agents who want to be asked for their order.

If they seem to be this type of buyer, if they look interested, and if the time is right, why not simply ask for the order?

"Mr. Smith your needs are a wonderful Fit-4-the capabilities of Acme Corporation. We are excited that your current widget promulgation will phase transition with Acme's metamorphosis capabilities. All of us at Acme will work hard to make your program a success. May we have an order?"

When things seem tough, or unsure, my personal favorite close is simply "What would you like me to do next?"

"Mr. Smith your needs are a wonderful Fit-4-the capabilities of Acme Corporation. We are excited that your current widget promulgation will phase transition with Acme's metamorphosis capabilities. All of us at Acme will work hard to make your program a success. What would you like us to do next?"

Chapter 2 – Marketing Strategies

Read this carefully because this is the key to all market strategies. When your sales force closes sales, they will do so, only by understanding your customer's emotions. Your customers will buy from China, India, South America, anybody. Very few industrial customers have loyalty to any country, or brand name, today. If you don't agree, just look at number of people drinking bottled water that is imported from other countries.

The last time I looked, the United States did produce good clean water. Go Figure.

You must understand your customer's psychological needs. Take a piece of paper out and write this down, "You must understand your customer's psychological needs to best succeed, in product marketing and sales." This is how to do it:

If Possible, Do Market Testing: Show product and promotional concepts to customers.

Make Strategy Decisions: Decide on new revenue growth and profits. Decide on new product development. Decide on price. Decide on sales force, distribution, and service. Decide on customer psychological factors, not features and benefits. Decide on product promotion.

A popular way to remember the function of marketing are the "four p's of marketing", which are product (you must have a "new product development process"), place (distribution, or where you will sell your product), promotion, and price.

A good definition of marketing will provide a more detailed definition of the standard marketing function, and the four p's of marketing. I added psychological sales factors as a fifth p of marketing; because, your marketing strategy must list the relevant sales psychology factors, and state how these factors will be addressed. Sales psychology is arguably the most important part of a marketing strategy.

Yet, customer psychology is seldom mentioned in marketing strategies.

Write An Action Plan: This involves a perk chart on product development - a calendar of planned media - a budget

Implement Your Plan: Hold routine meetings to review progress on sales leads. Provide a lead tracking system. Nothing is status quo. Revisit your plan and update it.

Ideas for your product marketing and sales efforts can be difficult to create: Start from basic marketing ideas. Then, apply your creative time to refine or modify those ideas to work best for your market!

• Take a customer to lunch, to play golf, to see a hockey game. It is a small token of thanks for their business, a great opportunity to hear about their level of satisfaction, and new opportunities. For example, in December, one company serves lunch to their customer's entire plant.

• Call your best customers. Need a reason? Think of one. I'm not being sarcastic. Think of a reason. Do not procrastinate on this. Call your best customers, often, but not too often.

• Meet with your largest customers at least two times each year, or better, once a quarter. A good agenda might be something along the lines of a "quality review". Present your company's improvements and actions taken to improve products, or correct past problems. Let your customer ask questions and voice their opinions and ideas.

• Starving for a good question to ask a satisfied repeat customer? "Is there anything else that our organization could do for you that we are not?" and "Is there anything that you think our organization should plan for in the future?"

• Do not forget about your vendors. Vendor relationships are critically important to your marketing and sales efforts. They should be second on your list, after customers. Vendors are a wonderful source of real-time marketing intelligence. Who's meeting with your competitors? Your vendors are meeting with your competitors. Thus, you need to meet with your vendors. Talk with your vendors. Build strong relationships with them -- the very kind of relationships you dream your customers would build with you.

•   Looking for a future? Find a lasting competitive advantage in your marketing strategy. Maybe it's a secret manufacturing procedure? A distributor network? A patent? Whatever. But, do not, ever, tell your vendors about your secret competitive advantages.

•   Postcards. They cost little to mail, are particularly interesting, when creative, and are a great way to say 'hello' to your current customers. For example, one company put a photo, of all of their employees, on one side of the card. The other side asked the customer for their next order.

•   Ask each of your employees to write down 20 new product ideas. The first 15 ideas rarely offer much. The last couple of ideas can be surprising. (Try it yourself -- the struggle of thinking of the last few ideas isn't as easy as you might think, and sparks creativity).

•   Before you call a customer to discuss your approach to a complicated problem, make a few notes on what you plan to say. During a potentially emotional discussion, these notes will serve to ground your approach.

•   Do you have a customer who is not happy, and won't say why? Is he is afraid of hurting your feelings? Try asking this way, "Is there anything that we could do a little bit better for you, that might make your life a little easier? Even the smallest thing?" Get ready to keep your mouth completely shut, and to write lots of notes.

- Go beyond "open ended questions" to get your prospect talking. Try stating a fact (perhaps something you saw in the morning paper), followed by a perception gleaned from that fact, followed by your question. For example, "A distributor told me today that plastic prices are increasing. It would seem that molding efficiency would be more critical, in this industry, than ever. How will it affect you?"

- On a shoestring budget? You might be shocked to learn how much marketing information is available for free at a good library. The trick today, might be finding a good business library! Try looking in universities or large cities. The business section in the Philadelphia Public Library, in Philadelphia, is an outstanding example. The last time I checked, they provided free access to several particularly expensive business databases.

- Cold calling is a tough, but effective tool of business-to-business marketing, and requires careful goal setting. Get started by working backward from an acceptable year-end result. For example, you may know, from experience that you will require about 40 new prospect meetings, during the next 12 months. You reason that you'll need to talk with 600 prospects, on the phone, to get those meetings. On the other hand, four out of five phone calls probably won't want to talk with you. Thus, you must call 3,000 prospects, during the 200 workday year. Now you have a goal: Call at least 15 prospects per day. If you do not have time, then make cold calling 2 prospects each morning, part of your daily discipline.

- Put this next to your phone: An index card with several issues about your market that you wish to better understand. Take it with you to meetings, or to trade events. Whenever you wish you to spice-up a conversation, admit that you are confused by one of the issues. Everyone likes to help -- not too different than asking for the time. You get lots of answers; and it all makes great conversation!

• Send a simple sales letter to all of your smaller customers, who haven't purchased lately (you should be talking to your large customers). The letter can say virtually anything. Perhaps it might read, in the first paragraph: It's fall; the leaves are turning, and our market is exciting! Our product development group has developed new widget interfaces that install faster than ever. Improved logic processors are now available for all of our IT800 series widgets. Call us, and our sales group will explain what's new for your IT800. Second paragraph: We have a new widget, the IT900, which has tripled our customers' line speeds in preliminary testing. Our "try IT" program allows you to buy the first IT900, for 15% off, until December 31st. Final paragraph: This update on Acme is also a reminder that you have not placed an order with us for some time. Everyone at Acme is hoping that you will consider us for your next order. If you have any questions, please don't hesitate to call. We look forward to assisting you.

• Quick Ship. Do you market products that are customized in some aspect? Consider carrying inventory of popular or common items. Then advertise the quick shipment of 'stock items'. This may have the added value of more efficient production.

• Develop a list of trade shows in your market. Make sure you visit several trade shows each year and learn. If you have ruled out exhibiting at a large national show, consider a smaller show, within driving distance. Many offer a "table top area," which is a great opportunity to use some creativity to put together a simple, but elegant exhibit.

• Install contact manager software on an internal network (it's not difficult to network a few computers). There are two or three major brands of software available in your local office supply store, many other brands as well. The important thing is to use one. When a customer calls in, they want an immediate response. With contact management software, you will be able to see records ~~on~~ of your associate's notes, past conversations, quotes, and promises. Long gone are the old days of, "Jim is on vacation. He will be back Monday. Can I take a message?" No thank you.

• Need to handle an angry customer? One who will not listen? One who will not understand your issues? The first rule is to let them talk! (Most sales people become anxious, and try to jump in too soon with a solution.) In fact, keep them talking until they know you understand, and until they have said everything that they need to say. A complaint will come in waves. Repeat the problem after each wave, and acknowledge their emotion; "I can understand why you are angry". Continue along these lines until the customer is completely finished. Then, he will be more responsive to your efforts to help.

The definition of strategic marketing is usually divided into four functional areas. You may notice that my definition of marketing includes having something for people to buy, finding people who will buy it, encouraging people to buy, and providing value-building benefits. Together, these objectives form a picture of strategic marketing.

"You cannot trust dogs to watch your food."

(You are in charge of your own conduct and as such are responsible for keeping yourself moral, and ethical.)

Chapter 3 – Market Objectives

To more easily remember these market objectives, marketing is more often described as "The Four P's":

- **Product**
- **Place**
- **Promotion**
- **Price**
- **Product: That concept which may be sold.**

The word product qualifies a marketing concept. A product is more than a person, place or thing. Nothing is more important to a marketing strategy than the "product concept".

In fact, finding the right product concept is one of the four critical objectives of marketing. The following example illustrates why the successful strategic marketer will carefully and completely consider his product options.

Swiss watch companies made 'Swiss watch actions,' and enjoyed a dominant position in the world market. By the 1970's, they had introduced many inventive variations of the 'Swiss watch action'. However, they completely ignored the streams of independent invention that, together, created the quartz watch movement.

During the early 1900's, aerospace scientists invented new materials like liquid crystals, and laid the basis for miniaturized electronic circuitry, calculators -- and watches.

The number of employees making Swiss watch actions fell from 90,000 in 1970 to 30,000 in 1980 (the number of companies decreased from 1,600 to only 600). The effect is significant: Still, today, only 35,000 employees manufacture Swiss watch actions.

Aggressive marketers believe that continuous product development is the most important of all strategic marketing activities.

Place: A gathering where people buy and sell
Place can mean geographic and demographic, or in others words, where and who. It can also be the way you take your product to the market (distribution).

Small companies often find a specialized place to sell (often referred to as a 'niche') as an effective way to overcome huge competitors, who easily overlook 5% of their market.

By the way, "market segmentation" refers to the very specific identification and understanding of these 'places', what they want, and how they buy it.

Promotion: The process of trading in a market

Ultimately, you will be ready to promote your product, find new prospects, and draw them in. The types of promotion that are available, to the strategic marketer, have not changed much, since the invention of the telephone (telemarketing).

But, there has been an amazing amount of new creative ways of applying the fundamentals to best suit products and market segments. Can you think of appropriate and creative ways to apply the fundamentals? (See below)

Space advertising (magazine, internet), direct advertising (postal, email), telemarketing, personal sales (sales people, reps), public relations (press releases, speeches), media advertising (television, radio), billboards (highway signs, hallway posters, blimps), road shows (tradeshows, craft shows), incentives (tee-shirts, awards, vacations, contests), discounts (sales, coupons)

Before selecting a promotional avenue, many marketers will first decide on Product, Price and Place. Try to understand who your prospects are, and why they buy. Review their budget and risk level.

After doing at least that much, decide on appropriate promotional avenues, that make sense. Finally, decide on creative ways to apply promotional programs. Personally, I think it's often a mistake to do what many do, and begin with the creative work first.

Price: To sell in a market
A market price has nothing to do with you, or your company.

A graduate professor, in Financial Management, taught us several different ways to precisely determine the cost of a product.

Then he asked the class, "Ok, we have an example of a company that manufactures a product that costs $1.00. At what price can this company sell the product?"

Out came the calculators, "For $1.65. For this particular company, that will cover the cost of taxes, goods sold, manufacturing, overhead, marketing, depreciation, and still provide a 5% net income, which is slightly better than the average in this particular market!"

The professor calmly stated, "No."

"You may sell your product at any price the customer is willing to pay.

Determine where your competitors are most vulnerable."

Chapter 4 – The History Part of Strategy

Direct Action!

While writing the history, you will focus on extracting and assembling your competitor analysis, by building a framework of their history, goals, strategies, beliefs, and capabilities. Do your market research; and, write your market history while keeping this objective in mind.

History: This history, of your industry, is a key component of understanding your current situation, the trends and forward possibilities.

Goals: From your history, you may begin to assemble obvious competitor goals. This is basically a summary of how competitors are currently operating in your industry. Your assumptions about future goals take on significance and understanding. Try to understand their assumption of risk, their corporate values, and their long-term commitments.

Strategy: From goals, you begin to understand your competitor's strategies. This is a synopsis of what competitors are trying to accomplish, and move toward. Do they typically use head-on attacks, or "jungle" warfare?

Beliefs: What do your competitors believe? What are the differences between competitor beliefs? Are competitor's beliefs uniform, or are they different, in your industry? How have these beliefs changed over time? Can you find gaps, or dogmatic misconceptions?

Capabilities: As the history unfolds, you will be better able to understand their capabilities, and understand how these have changed over time. Can you understand their financial resources? Will they be able to sufficiently respond to the changes in the paradigm that you create?

Use this history, and your analysis of it, to determine where the market is vulnerable, and where it might offer your organization the most opportunity. Here's an example:

A street has competitive gas stations. The street runs toward a major city, and is a perfect location for daily commuters, who demand gasoline.

At the start, there was plenty of demand for every gas station. Over many years, new competitive gas stations were built. In response, the existing stations switched to using computerized self-serve, to improve their competitive cost position.

Price wars continued, until all stations were barely profitable. Most believed that they could lower their prices, while their property values increased. Their competitors would be driven to financial failure, having to pay the interest burdens, which they acquired, purchasing new property.

Meanwhile, the existing stations would pay their property taxes, and meet their costs, while planning to sell their property, for a profit, in later years. The strategic situation looked bleak for the newer stations that wished to make a net income -- except for one.

Here the history shows market goals of surviving price wars. The marketing strategy is to survive with the lowest possible price, to sell property, in some later year, for a profit. The market belief is that gas stations provide gasoline, which is a commodity.

Obviously, there is no "value added" aspect of a gas station. Market capabilities were increasingly focused on small stores, with low overhead costs, that focused on efficient computerized self-service gasoline.

One owner decided to be different. He reinstated full service.

In fact, he instated more than service; he instated incredible service.

A market segment came to his store, for the better service.

He bought his neighbor's station, and merged the two facilities.

He built an elaborate store, with high quality fast food service. He used an architect to design a light, brightly colored, recognizable building.

He used the increased customer volume to leverage vendors, and to receive lower prices on gas -- increasing his profits.

Can you imagine the strategy and mission statement of this new player? Can you imagine that this company was successful? Can you imagine that they could possibly have "stations," covering the entire United States, today?

Keep this in mind; a competitor analysis should focus on where competitors are most vulnerable. Write a history of your industry and your competitors. This will help to challenge your assumptions, and keep your thoughts organized and sane, while you analyze a difficult situation.

Let' talk about water...In this case, the marketing challenge was to create a unique selling proposition for water. We saw how one person wanted to promote the safety of clean water, and its excellent benefits.

But, does clean, safe water need to be shipped across the world? Hahahaha! The creative genius here, was to find the idea to associate "taste and style," with water.

Brilliant!

Can you be creative with your own product, to find a way to promote its true strengths? Sure you can! As always, sales and marketing research finds that emotions are the most powerful motivators.

Now that you know how to promote water as having "taste and style", can you find an elegant brand name to strengthen the emotion you want for your product? What kind of packaging should you use?

Will it impress your customer's friends? Keep in mind that it is important to creatively associate a positive emotion and positive attitude with your product. All of this must be believable, so that, "product features and benefits" are assumed -- you don't need to individually list them.

Let Me Repeat That: Keep in mind that it is important to creatively associate a positive emotion and positive attitude with your product. All of this must be believable, so that "product features and benefits" are assumed -- you don't need to individually list them. Then, your branding work may be successful.

"People want the front of the bus, the back of the church and the center of attention."

(Everyone wants to be a Big Shot)

Chapter 5 – Using Psychology to Boost Sales

If you want to be truly successful in sales, you need to take a close look at how psychology can set you apart from the rest of your competition. Dynamic Psychology can be applied to all aspects of your marketing efforts, and will give you that vital edge over your competitors.

All-Time Secrets of Negotiating: Remember this: no matter how great your product or service, unless you can negotiate innovatively, you'll never achieve the success that can rightly be yours. When you approach prospects, ask them if you can explore how your mutual expertise (experience), can benefit both sides. This is very powerful from a psychological point of view, because you are telling prospects that you want to understand their needs. **Seek first to understand, then to be understood.**

"A buyer with an argument is ALWAYS at the mercy of a salesperson with experience."

How To Make People Respond More Quickly: Remember this:

"People respond more to what they are going to lose,

than to what they are going to gain."

It's very powerful when you explain to prospects they will probably lose market share, to their main competitors, if they don't adopt your ideas. Ask yourself: What will my customers stand to lose if they do not buy my service or product?

KNOW YOUR PRODUCT!

EXPERIENCE CANNOT BE COUNTERED EFFECTIVELY!

Psychology can also play a powerful part in overcoming objections to requests for a sales meeting. There are two strategies that will result in incredible opportunities coming your way. Try them today.

1. Tell your prospects that you really want to understand their needs, precisely, and you feel that you can't achieve this, unless you talk to them in person. People want to feel understood more than anything else, and the salespeople who understand this, take all.

2. You can also add that it will only take, say, 12 minutes, (let them time you!) to show them how they can benefit from what you're offering. You can also offer to give them a free gift (low cost with a perceived high value); e.g., promotional travel vacations, reports, gift certificates, etc., if they think you've wasted their time.

The Greatest Packaging Secret Revealed:

Did you know that you'd increase your sales, by using appealing photographs of typical users, on your packaging? Why is this? Well, it humanizes your product or service, and prospects perceive you to be more professional and trustworthy.

How to Avoid the Biggest Mistake of All:
No matter what type of business you run, you must sell benefits, not features. If you sell your product or service, using features, you must stop this mistake immediately. Suppose you sell accommodations, you can sell its features: "Large rooms overlooking the sea with private facilities". How many advertisements do you see like this? If you sell benefits, you sell customers a lifestyle, and that's psychologically powerful.

For example, you can productize by offering "Romantic vacations" (your product), with a special offer of 5 nights, for the price of 4 (innovative pricing to encourage a larger sale). You can then detail why they are romantic: for example, free champagne on arrival, rooms with four-poster beds and whirlpool baths. The possibilities are endless, no matter what type of business you run. The secret is to turn your service or product into a package and combine it with innovative pricing. In a buyer's mind, features drive up the price of the product/service; however, a buyer perceives that benefits do not drive up the price, but are inherent built-in value.

How to Price for Profit:
Let's take a closer look at pricing for success. Psychologists tell us that prices ending in "7," sell more than prices ending in "9". For example, $1.97 will probably be more powerful than $1.99. Do you use this technique? Test it and see. Do be aware that, if you sell a

prestigious product or service, this will "cheapen" its image, so avoid this strategy for expensive products.

You can also lower your price if customers buy larger quantities; for instance, $40 for one, or $97 for three.

Another powerful psychological pricing strategy is using a technique that appears to lower the cost of your product. For example, if you charge $500 per year for your service, you could offer it for "less than $10 per week".

It's the same price eventually, (remember debt service!); however, can you see why this is more appealing? Ten dollars will attract more immediate attention than a whopping $500.

"When you throw a rock into a pack of dogs, the one that yelps is the one that got hit."

(Keep making sales calls)

Chapter 6 – Beating Your Competition Without Cutting Your Price

One way to beat your competition is to charge less, for a similar product or service. But, you can also beat your competition when your price is higher. One of the best ways to avoid price competition is to become a specialist in a narrowly defined targeted market.

Relating Is More Important Than Pricing:

Recently, I spoke with the creator of a marketing program for new business owners. He could have confronted the established competition, and competed with a lower price. Instead he decided to target prospects in 2 types of businesses he had worked with before -- insurance sales and MLM marketing. He knew a lot about the operation of each business, and the people who worked in them. He created a separate web site for each type of business, and customized the content to appeal specifically to prospects in that business. The site for insurance sales people looked the same as the site for MLM marketers. But, the content was totally different. His plan worked. Sales are running almost 50 percent, ahead of projection ...even with a price that's 15 percent higher than similar programs. He built a successful business, in a highly competitive market, by becoming a specialist.

Customers Like To Buy From A Specialist: People like to do business with a specialist, who has a unique insight into their situation. They feel confident about getting what they expect, from a product or service, when somebody who understands them and their unique needs, proposes it. Most customers, or clients, will even pay a little more to buy from somebody who thinks like them. It's worth it to avoid the risk of being disappointed, because they bought from somebody who didn't know anything about their special situation.

You'll Sell More As A Specialist: Targeting a niche market, enables you to design your sales messages with great precision. You can cater to specifically defined interests of prospects, and communicate with them in their own style. More people will buy when they feel you are talking directly to them about their individual needs. Special Benefit: Delivering results as a specialist, establishes you as an expert in your field. Customers and prospects will automatically refer their associates, and other prospects, to you. They value what you have done for them. And, they're confident you can do the same thing for others in a similar situation.

Simple Steps to Becoming a Specialist: Becoming a specialist is easier than you may think. You can accomplish it in 3 simple steps:

1. Divide your primary market into several narrowly defined markets.

2. Take each market, one at a time, and learn everything you can about the prospects in it.

3. Revise your marketing approach and selling materials to appeal to the specific needs of prospects in each new market. Use the customer's own unique language and style of communication.

Tip: Existing customers, who match the profile of prospects, in a market you've targeted, can help you develop your sales approach for that market. Contact some of them and ask them why they bought your product or service. What do they like best about it? Why did they choose you instead of a competitor? They'll give you a lot of information that you can use, to develop your appeal to other prospects like them. You'll always have competitors. But, you don't have to lower your price to compete with them. Instead, become a specialist and cater to prospects in a narrowly defined, targeted market. Your understanding and insight, into their unique situation, will establish you as the expert in your field. They'll want to do business with YOU, even if you don't offer the lowest price.

Chapter 7 – Observation

What I am about to teach you is, without a doubt, one of the most important art forms to learn. The art of observing, involves seeing and listening. But, it goes much farther than that. Many people hear and see but, PERCEIVE what they hear and see as something totally different than what was meant.

As a scientist, I am trained to observe. It is the most important tool a person, in my trade, must possess. When I speak to people, and I am unsure of what they MEANT, I ask this question, "Let me see if I understand you correctly?" or "Let me see if I am seeing what you seeing?" My company uses a technique to train our staff to observe. This is how we do it:

To teach people to see: Take a blank wall (it must be blank), and sit in front of this wall with a pen and pad. Write down a hundred things about the wall. At first, you will find this very difficult. The usual response is, "It's just a wall". Write it down! What color is the wall? Write it down! What texture is it - its shape, does it have any blemishes on it, what is it a part of, etc? You will find, when you are finished, that you have written down over a hundred characteristics of that "blank wall," as you begin to see it more and more. We do the same in teaching people to listen:

To teach people to listen: Sit in a park with a pen and pad. Listen to every sound around you, and write down a hundred sounds you hear. You will be amazed at the amount of sound information your brain takes in and discards.

Now, why do people not hear or see so many things? It is simply a matter of selfish pursuit. When you become so wrapped up in your daily existence, and your life, you tend to filter out incoming stimuli. But, it goes farther than this too. Most, if not everybody, fantasizes whenever they can "get-away". This fantasy life can become very dangerous when a person chooses to live within their fantasy. Whenever you allow yourself to become distracted, with daydreaming, or fantasy, your brain automatically filters out anything that would distract you from this selfish pursuit. The outside stimuli are there to teach you what the world is telling you. By creating your own fantasy world, you actually block out reality. Please don't do this!

Now, let's talk about PERCEIVED observation, versus actual observation. In group sessions that I have with women, the topic of weight control always seems to become an issue. Since, I am also a nutritionist, and the physical body has quite a lot to do with the mental aspects of men and women, this is something that I'm confronted with, quite often. In one session, a particularly striking and beautiful woman made the remark that she was always struggling with her weight. The other women in the group would have cut off body parts to have the physical attributes of this woman, and they were quite vocal in telling her so; I might add. However, I asked her to explain herself. She told the group that (in her mind); if she wasn't careful, she could easily gain two pounds, just looking at food. Well, the whole group erupted after that statement. The other women did not care about two measly pounds. But, this woman perceived this to be **her** problem. The others in the group heard what she said, but filtered out what she meant. She meant that she always had to be conscious of her food intake, EVEN though she based weight gain on such a paltry scale, in comparison to the other women. To the other women, she was ridiculous, and not worth listening to after that.

We need to listen and observe what is actually happening; not allow so much of it to run through our internal filters, perceiving it as something it isn't. Understanding this is critical, when asking a customer about their needs. Probing questions are so very important, but listening to the responses, that is equally important... Here is an example:

An insurance client of mine had an appointment with the Chief Executive Officer of a very large company. Because of the size of the policy involved, the sales manager requested I be a part of the sale, from beginning to end. The account executive was a fine young saleswoman, with a track record of very large sales. This sale, involved a retirement policy. Our initial appointment went very well. The buyer, a male, listened closely to what the saleswomen was asking.

46

One of her questions was, "Mr. X, how much will you need monthly, when you retire?" and she stopped there.

He answered her question the way it was asked (which is a typical male response), "I will need about $10,000 per month."

This is what she did wrong: In the news recently, retirement plans of all kinds, have witnessed a tremendous drop in value because of the drop in the stock market. This has caused a good deal of stress and anxiety for people who rely on their retirement and pension plans.

One of the questions the saleswoman had asked the executive, while "fact-finding," was about his existing pension plan, which he described in detail. When he told her he needed $10,000 per month, she wrongly assumed this is what he was asking, of the policy, she would offer to provide. This was not true.

I jumped in and asked the following question: "Mr. X, will the policy we provide, supplement your current pension plan, or would you like us to provide a policy that will pay out $10,000 each month?" The answer was what I expected. This new policy was to "supplement" his existing plan. The saleswoman would have gone back to her office, and put together a program that paid out $10,000 per month. The executive would have turned it down.

Learning to probe, and asking the right questions, is another art form. Learning what I teach you here, when dealing with a male or female buyer, is important. Men answer questions literally, where female buyers imply many things. A female buyer, using the example of the situation above, may have responded like this:

"Ms. X, how much will you need monthly, when you retire?"

"I will need enough to cover my personal expenses plus, some leisure money."

"Fine, I understand, but do you have a figure in mind?"

"Not really, I haven't given any thought to a figure, but I do know that what the company provides isn't going to be enough, and I cannot even rely on that."

"I can most certainly agree with you. Ms. X, how much will you receive from your company plan?"

"Approximately $7500 per month, that's assuming the stock market doesn't destroy it."

"Yes, unfortunately you are right about that. What I will do is go back to my office, and put together a program based on three supplemental figures, so you will have the option to choose what monthly amount is best for you. Will this be okay with you?"

"Yes, I would like that!"

The difference in the above discourse, compared to the male buyer, was that the female executive gave numerous clues to her needs. She was more specific, where the male buyer kept a good deal of information to himself, and it needed to be "probed out" of him.

She would not commit to a monthly figure (she knew exactly what she needed), and wanted the saleswoman to present her with options, in order to validate this figure. Women like to shop; men do not. Men are bottom line shoppers; women are not.

Always listen to what is being said, but also, always listen to what is not being said. Be sure you understand your customer's needs, and always ask, "I think that just about does it. Have I missed anything?" Then listen to what the customer says.

Observation also includes body language. This involves a separate class, and is too involved to discuss here. But, understand, that by observing a customer's body language, a salesperson has a window into the customer's psyche.

There, bodily responses give away their mental thoughts. It is easy to see if a customer is listening to you and finding value and worth in what you are saying.

I Have a Special Gift for My Readers

I appreciate my readers for without them I am just another author attempting to make a difference. If my book has made a favorable impression please leave me an honest review.   Thank you in advance for you participation.

My readers and I have in common a passion for the written word as well as the desire to learn and grow from books.

My special offer to you is a massive ebook library that I have compiled over the years. It contains hundreds of fiction and non-fiction ebooks in Adobe Acrobat PDF format as well as the Greek classics and old literary classics too.

In fact, this library is so massive to completely download the entire library will require over 5 GBs open on your desktop.

Use the link below and scan all of the ebooks in the library. You can select the ebooks you want individually or download the entire library.

The link below does not expire after a given time period so you are free to return for more books rather than clog your desktop. And feel free to give the link to your friends who enjoy reading too.

I thank you for reading my book and hope if you are pleased that you will leave me an honest review so that I can improve my work and or write books that appeal to your interests.

Okay, here is the link…

http://tinyurl.com/special-readers-promo

PS: If you wish to reach me personally for any reason you may simply write to mailto:support@epubwealth.com.

Meet the Author

Dr. Harry Jay is Director of Research for AppliedMindSciences.com, a mental health and mind research group of Applied Web Info, and is the author of over 100 books and research papers as a behavioral scientist.

In his 32-year career, Dr. Harry Jay has contributed many new mental health treatment treatments and protocols using some of the new advances he has discovered in Energy Psychology.

He specializes in addictions of all kinds, sexual abuse, child predation and gender relationships.

He is also a board member to ePubWealth.com and serves on the science committee assisting non-fiction science writers in book publishing and promotion.

As a leading behavioral scientist, he provides profiling services to the company's ForensicsNation.com unit as well as criminal psychology research to aid in identifying and apprehending child predators and cyber-criminals of all kinds.

He resides in Southern Utah and enjoys the outdoors, fishing and photography.

Visit some of his websites

http://www.AddMeInNow.com
http://www.AppliedMindSciences.com
http://www.BookbuilderPLUS.com
http://www.BookJumping.com
http://www.EmailNations.com
http://www.EmbarrassingProblemsFix.com
http://www.ePubWealth.com
http://www.ForensicsNation.com
http://www.ForensicsNationStore.com
http://www.FreebiesNation.com
http://www.HealthFitnessWellnessNation.com
http://www.Neternatives.com
http://www.PrivacyNations.com
http://www.RetireWithoutMoney.org
http://www.SurvivalNations.com
http://www.TheBentonKitchen.com
http://www.Theolegions.org
http://www.VideoBookbuilder.com

www.ingramcontent.com/pod-product-compliance
Lightning Source LLC
Chambersburg PA
CBHW051822170526

45167CB00005B/2113